Welcome to Uncle Eli's Haggadah.

The idea for this book goes back many years ago, to a two-year-old boy who loved celebrating the Jewish holidays almost as much as he loved listening to the silly rhymes in his children's books. For his sake, I decided to combine those two things: I tried to tell the story of the Passover Seder in the style of his beloved children's books, in verse and with help from lots of zany characters and creatures.

Soon we found that other children enjoyed it just as much, and so did their parents. We added colorful pictures, and now offer Uncle Eli's Haggadah to you. We hope you will enjoy it as we have.

If you already know about Passover, the "Haggadah," and the "Seder," then this little book should add to your fun, as it presents the Jewish holiday traditions in its unique and enjoyable style.

If you have never experienced a Seder, or if you found it dull and boring, then this will be a pleasant new introduction. When you run into strange words, try looking them up in the glossary at the back of the book.

I hope that Uncle Eli's Haggadah will help make this Passover your happiest one ever.

Eliezer Segal

UNCLE ELI'S
Special-for-Kids
Most Fun Ever
Under-the-Table
PASSOVER HAGGADAH

Uncle Eli's
Special-for-Kids
Most Fun Ever
Under-the-Table
Passover Haggadah
הגדה של פסח

By Eliezer Segal

Illustrated by
Bonnie Gordon-Lucas

NO STARCH PRESS
SAN FRANCISCO

For the children and teachers of the Akiva Academy, Calgary

Printed in Hong Kong
ISBN 1–886411–26–3 (paperback)
ISBN 1–886411–27–1 (cloth)

Library of Congress Cataloging-in-Publication Data available.

Distributed to the book trade in the United States and Canada by
Publishers Group West, 1700 Fourth Street, Berkeley, California 94710, U.S.A.

10 9 8 7 6 5 4 3 2 1

No Starch Press
555 De Haro Street, Suite 250, San Francisco, California 94107, U.S.A.

TABLE OF CONTENTS

A Present from Uncle Eli

The house had gone crazy,
    all turned upside-down,
with everyone busily
    running around.
Mommy was screaming,
    "Get out of the way!
You can't keep on
    lying around here all day!
Tomorrow is Passover.
    You don't look ready.
We have to remove
    everything that is bready.
Pack up the old dishes
    and pull out the new.
Prepare for the Seder!
    There's too much to do!"

I just stuffed up my ears,
    'cause I'm that kind of kid.
I didn't much care
    what the rest of them did.
I thought it was stupid;
    I felt it was dumb

to get so excited
      about one or two crumbs
when under my bed,
      under careful protection,
I keep the world's largest
      stale breadcrumb collection!
I hate cleaning up.
      I prefer a good mess.
I'm lazy and mean—
      kind of nasty, I guess.
I don't like the Seder.
      It bores me to tears.
I sit making faces
      and noises and sneers.

I'd rather be out
        breaking windows with balls,
or digging up flowerbeds,
        or drawing on walls.
Anything! Anywhere
        rather than be
at the Passover Seder
        with my family.
We mean little kids
        should be sent away.
We don't want to celebrate
        these dumb holidays.

Well, those were the thoughts
        spinning inside my head.
My ears were exploding,
        my nose had turned red.
I was very upset
        at my mom and my dad—
disgusted, disgruntled
        —in short, I was mad!

When . . .

right there behind me
        I heard a soft sound.
I perked up my ears
        and I turned my head 'round.
And standing before me,
        as plain as could be
was the weirdest old man
        that you ever will see.
"Weird" did I say?
        He was weirder than weird!
You hardly could see him
        because of his beard.

It flowed down his body
        and covered his feet,
all curly and snaggly,
        distinctly un-neat.
Aside from that beard—
        well, you couldn't see lots,
just two twinkly eyes
        that peeked out 'tween the knots,
and the hint of a grin
        that made everything bright
and sometimes turned into
        a laughing white light.

I stared at this strange little man
        for a while
as he kept standing there
        full of laughter and smiles.
The door to the room
        was still shut up tight,
and I didn't know how
        he had gotten inside.

I finally got up the nerve
        to speak out:
"You are a strange fellow,
        without any doubt.
Please, tell me who are you?
        And why are you here?
And why do you look
        so fantastically queer?"

He lit up his smile
 and began to reply:
"It is me, your old friend,
 Uncle Eli am I!

And I, Uncle Eli,
        am just the right one
to make sure that this year
        you will have lots of fun.
Instead of just sitting there
        twiddling your hands
while the grown-ups read words
        that you don't understand,
I've brought you
        a special Haggadah to read.
It'll keep you in stitches!
        It's just what you need!
I wrote it for children
        like you and your friends,
who hardly can wait
        for the Seder to end.
It's just the right thing
        for a silly young boy—
a Haggadah you'll learn
        to adore and enjoy."

Then, waving his finger
        and wiggling his ears,
he stuck his right hand
        in his tangled white beard.
From somewhere down deep
        in that jungle of hair
he pulled out a book,
        which he held in the air.

It's the same fun Haggadah
        you're reading today.
Don't let your folks see it!
        They'll take it away.
You might want to hide it
        where no one can see,
under the table,
        on top of your knee.
It'll be our own secret.
        They won't understand
why you cover your mouth
        with the back of your hand
to stifle the laughs
        that burst out all the time.
It's your own special secret,
                and Eli's
                        . . . and mine!

Bedikat Hametz

בדיקת חמץ

We have to get rid
    of the hametz today—
We have to destroy it.
    We can't let it stay.

We'll punch it and crunch it
      and bury it deep,
or leave it to rot
      on Mount Zeepleep-the-Steep.
We'll pump on it, jump on it,
      grind it to dust.
Erode it, corrode it—
      We have to! We must!
We'll feed it to ravenous
      rampaging rhinos—or
trample it all
      on our dizzy old dinosaur.
Cut it to pieces,
      and burn it to ash!
Bash it and smash it
      and dash it to hash.
Then send it by rocket
      to the Forests of Queet,
where fire-breathing Goo-bahs
      will turn on the heat.
We'll sink it way down
      to the floor of the ocean
and finish it off
      with a mighty explosion.

We have to get rid
      of the hametz today—
We have to destroy it.
      We can't let it stay.

The Four Cups

ארבע כוסות

Jacky the juggler
    is four inches small,
but he'll juggle the four cups
    and not one will fall.
Each cup is filled up
    with red wine to its top.
They dance through the air
    but he won't spill a drop.

Sari is trying
      to tickle his toes,
and she's wiggling a feather
      right under his nose.
But Jacky keeps juggling.
      His eyes are now closed.
His feet in the air
      and one hand on the ground,
the four cups keep spinning
      around and around.
He sings through the Kiddush.
      He reads the Haggadah.
He's balancing now
      on the top of a ladder.
He's saying the Grace
      that we say after meals.
The cups are still spinning
      like wobbly wheels.
He's finished the Hallel,
      and started to snore,
but he still keeps on juggling,
      asleep on the floor.
They're dancing like ducklings,
      they're spinning like tops—
I don't think that Jacky-boy
      ever will stop.

Ha Lachma

הא לחמא

This is the poorest,
    the driest of bread.
It crinkles and crumbles
    all over our beds.
This is the matzah
    that Grand-Daddy ate
when he zoomed out of Egypt,
    afraid he'd be late.

You're welcome to join us—
    Come one or come many!
I'll give you my matzah.
    I sure don't want any.

The Four Questions

מה נשתנה

Why is it only
      on Passover night
we never know how
      to do anything right?
We don't eat our meals
      in the regular ways,
the ways that we do
      on all other days.

For on all other
      nights we may eat
all kinds of wonderful
      good bready treats,
like big purple pizza
      that tastes like a pickle,
crumbly crackers
      and pink pumpernickel,
sassafras sandwich
      and tiger on rye,*
fifty falafels
      in pita,
fresh-fried,
      with peanut butter
and tangerine sauce

* URGENT WARNING ABOUT TIGERS!! Please be advised that in spite of the impression created by this poem, tigers are not kosher animals, and may not be eaten according to Jewish religious law (even on rye)! They are also extremely dangerous. The reference here was apparently inserted by an unscrupulous prankster, or it refers to a vegetarian imitation, or maybe an ice-cream flavor.

spread onto each side
     up-and-down, then across,
and toasted whole-wheat bread
     with liver and ducks,
and crumpets and dumplings,
     and bagels and lox,
and doughnuts with one hole
     and doughnuts with four,
and cake with six layers
     and windows and doors.
Yes—
on all other nights
     we eat all kinds of bread,
but tonight of all nights
     we munch matzah instead.

On all other nights
     we are free to devour
vegetables, green things,
     and bushes and flowers,
lettuce that's leafy
     and candy-striped spinach,
salads of celery,
     (Have more when you're finished!)
cabbage that's flown
     from the jungles of Glome
by a polka-dot bird
     who can't find his way home,

daisies and roses
        and inside-out grass
and artichoke hearts
        that are simply first class!
Sixty asparagus tips
        served in glasses
with anchovy sauce
        and some sticky molasses—
But on Passover night
        you would never consider
eating an herb
        that wasn't all bitter.

And on all other nights
        you would probably flip
if anyone asked you
        how often you dip.
On some days I only dip
        one Bup-Bup egg
in a teaspoon of vinegar
        mixed with nutmeg,
but sometimes we take
        more than ten thousand tails
of the Yakkity-birds
        that are hunted in Wales,
and dip them in vats
        full of Mumbegum juice.

Then we feed them to Harold,
    our six-legged moose.
Or we don't dip at all—
    We don't ask your advice.
So why on this night
    do we have to dip twice?

And on all other nights
    we can sit as we please,
on our heads, on our elbows,
    our backs or our knees,

or hang by our toes
        from the tail of a Glump,
or on top of a camel
        with one or two humps,
with our foot on the table,
        our nose on the floor,
with one ear in the window
        and one out the door,
doing somersaults
        over the greasy knishes
or dancing a jig
        without breaking the dishes.
Yes—
on all other nights
        you sit nicely when dining—
So why on this night
        must it all be reclining?

Avadim Hayinu

עבדים היינו

We were slaves to King Pharaoh,
    that terrible king,
who made us do all kinds
    of difficult things.
Like building a pyramid
    of chocolate ice cream
when the sun was so hot
    that the Nile turned to steam,
and digging a ditch
    with a spade of soft cotton.
That Pharaoh was wicked
    and nasty and rotten!
He made us prepare him
    a big birthday cake
and buy fancy presents
    for Pharaoh to take,
He kept us awake
    with a terrible noise,
but never allowed us
    to play with his toys.

It's a good thing that God
    took us out of that place
and gave evil old Pharaoh
    a slap in the face.
Because if He hadn't,
    we'd all be in trouble,
still slaving away
    in the dust and the rubble,
cleaning up the king's mess
    and still folding his clothes,
and arranging his torn socks
    in eighty-four rows,
and balancing eggs
    on the tips of our toes.

Yes, even if we were
    as smart as my mother,
as wise as my best friend Dov's
    four-month-old brother,
if we'd read all the books
    in the public library
or watched as much TV
    as old Auntie Mary—
We still should keep telling
    this wonderful story
of how we got out
    in a huff and a hurry.

Ma'aseh B'Rabbi Eliezer

מעשה ברבי אליעזר

Once Rabbi Akiva
   and some of his friends
talked all night and forgot
   that the Seder should end.
All the mice started snoring,
   they found it so boring.
The hoot-owls were hooting,
   the shooting-stars shooting—
But Rabbi Akiva
   kept talking away
till his pupils said, "Rabbi,
   it's not yesterday!
You act like the Drush-Drush
   who sleeps while it's light,
and talks of the Exodus
   all through the night!"

Amar Rabbi Eleazar ben Azariah

אמר רבי אלעזר בן עזריה

Is there anyone sorrier
than Eleazar ben Azariah?
He thought it was right
to tell stories all night.
But ben Zoma was worse—
He could quote from a verse.
Now Eleazar looks seventy,
though he's not even twenty.
(Now I think that's plenty.)

The Four Children

כנגד ארבעה בנים

To our Seder last year
     came a strange-looking man
with four kids:
     Smarty,
     Nasty, and
     Simple, and
     Sam.
Now Smarty was smart—
     so clever and wise,
he could do the whole Seder
     while closing his eyes.
From beginning to end,
     from the end to the start,
he recited it
     over and over by heart.
In Hebrew and Hindi,
     in Snufic and Roman,
from the first Ha Lachma
     to the last Afikoman.

But Nasty refused
     to take part in the Seder.
He just sat there and smiled
     with his pet alligator
as he pulled people's hair
     and he poked people's eyes
and sprinkled their matzah
     with beetles and flies.

He certainly has
    quite a bad attitude.
If his fangs were less sharp,
    he might not be so rude.
If he'd been in Egypt
    complaining this way,
we'd have left him behind
    to keep slaving all day.

Away in the corner
    sits sweet sister Simple.
Whenever she smiles
    her face breaks out in dimples.
She only asks
    about simple facts
like "What is a matzah?"

and "Tell me how tall is a
Gloogasaurus Zax?"

Sam doesn't even
    know what to say.
He just sits in his box
    till the end of the day,
till his dad packs him up
    and takes him away.

Yakhol Me-Rosh Hodesh

יכול מראש חדש

The pigeon-toed, round-bellied,
    red-headed Bunth
starts his Seder on
    the first of the month.
But we think that Pesah
    is early enough.

The two-headed Dray
    has his Seder by day,
but we think it's just right
    to have it at night.

The Ten Plagues

עשר מכות

When Pharaoh got nasty
    and mean and deceiving
and wouldn't agree
    to the Israelites' leaving,
God sent him ten plagues
    so he might change his mind,
and the Jews could leave
    terrible Egypt behind.

There was
      blood in the gutters,
      and frogs in the butter,
      and lice on their heads,
      and beasts in their beds,
      disease in the cattle,
      and big boils in the saddle.
Hail started showering
      and locusts devouring.
It turned dark as a pit.
      Then the firstborn were hit.

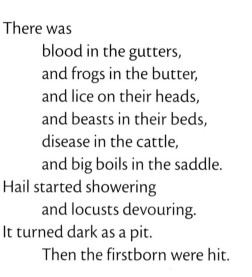

Rabban Gamliel Hayah Omer

רבן גמליאל היה אומר

Shh-h . . .
Rabban Gamliel
    has something to tell,
so we'd better all listen
    to him very well.

He says that each person
    must mention these three
if he wants his whole Seder
    to go perfectly.
Tonight these three things
    might be found in your parlor—
We know them as Pesah and matzah and maror.

Pesah, the lamb
　　that the Jews would prepare
at the time that the Temple
　　was still standing there,
to remind us of how
　　our ancestors were saved,
how they marched out of Egypt
　　and stopped being slaves.
It wasn't a soup
　　and it wasn't a stew.
It was more like roast lamb
　　in a big Bar-B-Q.
We try to remember
　　that lamb, if we're able,
by keeping a bone of some sort
　　on the table.

Matzah, this strange, flat,
　　and hard, crunchy bread
was the food that our forefathers ate
　　when they fled.
They didn't have time
　　to make something more tasty
like chocolate cake
　　or cherry-cream pastry,
because their departure was
　　ever so hasty.

The trip out of Egypt was
     all so haphazard,
they left mountains of matzah-crumbs
     all through the desert.
Manny, our matzah-dog,
     eats it by tons.
He'll have two hundred matzahs
     before the night's done.

The third thing is maror.
     These herbs are so bitter!
Let's give some to Marvin,
     our mean babysitter!

Zekher L'Mikdash K'Hillel

זכר למקדש כהלל

Hillel, while the Temple stood,
    made sandwiches he thought were good.
They had no jam or mozzarelly,
    tuna fish or vermicelli—
just matzah, maror, and some kind of meat.
    He thought they were a super treat
    (but there are lots of things
    I'd rather eat).

Afikoman

אֲפִיקוֹמָן

Do you know who I am?
    Have you heard of my name?
Once you have met me,
    you won't be the same.
I show up each year
    towards the end of the Seder.
My eyes see like telescopes,
    my ears have radar.

You can't ever fool me.
    You can't ever hide.
Your matzah's not safe
    in the house or outside.
I'm famous, fantastic!
    I'll tell you, in brief—
I'm Abie, the great Afikoman-thief!

Whenever you think
    that it's hidden away,
locked up in a safe,
    covered over in clay,
in the ear of a rabbit,
    the mouth of a whale—
I'll find it as quick
    as a wag of your tail.

Don't bother with watchers
        and guarders and catchers.
I'm Abie, the great Afikoman-snatcher!

I find Afikomans,
        no matter what size,
and I won't bring them back
        till you give me a prize.
I'm quick and I'm clever.
        I'm smart and I'm sly.
I hunt Afikomans
        wherever they lie.
In the trunk of a tree,
        in the nose of a rocket,
in the depths of a
        five-year-old boy's messy pocket.
You don't stand a chance.
        I'm beyond all belief.
I'm Abie, the great Afikoman-thief!

Opening the Door

As the Seder stretched on
        and I started to snore,
my mommy said, "Quick, now!
        Go open the door!"
I didn't know
        who would be coming right now,
but I stifled a yawn
        and I stood up somehow.
I walked to the door
        and I opened it wide,
and who do you think
        I saw standing outside?
My friend Uncle Eli
        with his beard to the floor
was waiting there quietly
        next to the door!
His eyes were still twinkling,
        his smile still bright.
He asked, "Are you having
        a good time tonight?"

I wanted to tell him
about all the fun
I'd been having
since this special night had begun.
But just as I opened
my mouth to reply,
he was gone, disappeared,
in the wink of an eye!
And I heard my mom calling:
"Come back in right now!
We already have welcomed
in Eliyahu—

"Eliyahu shows up
        at our Seder tonight
to make sure that
        everything's going all right.
He'll answer the questions
        we can't figure out.
He'll solve all our problems
        and settle our doubts.
He also will taste
        from the wine in his cup,
and we hope that this year
        he will cheer us all up,
by bringing us
        happy and wonderful news
of a year full of freedom
        in store for the Jews."

Uncle Eli's Glossary

AFIKOMAN   The very last thing that is eaten at the Seder is a piece of matzah called the *Afikoman*. In order to keep the children awake and attentive, it is customary for them to "steal" it and refuse to give it back unless their parents promise them a small gift. Sometimes the parents hide it and offer a reward to the child who finds it.

BEDIKAT HAMETZ (The Search for Leaven)   Because it is forbidden to have any hametz in the house during Passover, the house is thoroughly cleaned and checked beforehand. On the evening before the holiday, it is customary to search the house (traditionally, with a candle) to make sure that all the hametz has been removed. Whatever is left is set aside to be destroyed (usually by burning) the following morning. In Hebrew, this checking for hametz is called *Bedikat Hametz*.

BEN ZOMA   An ancient Jewish teacher who found a place in the Bible that speaks about reciting the Passover story at night.

BITTER HERBS (in Hebrew: *maror*)   To remember the bitterness of slavery, bitter herbs (usually lettuce or horseradish) are eaten at the Seder.

DIPPING   At the beginning of the Seder meal, different foods are eaten by dipping them in other items (celery in salt water, maror in a sweet paste called *haroset*). In ancient times, this was done only at fancy feasts attended by free people, and therefore it symbolizes freedom.

ELIJAH THE PROPHET (in Hebrew: *Eliyahu Ha-Navi*)   Elijah was one of the most beloved prophets of the Bible. He delivered messages from God, and miraculously helped many people. Elijah never actually died, but was taken up to Heaven in a flaming chariot. Therefore it is believed that he still travels around carrying messages between Heaven and Earth. The Bible also says that Elijah will be sent to announce the coming of the final redemption, when we will all live in a perfect and peaceful world. It is customary to leave a special cup of wine for Elijah on the Seder table, and it is believed that he takes a sip from it as he visits every house on Passover.

EXODUS   When the Israelites left the slavery of Egypt.

THE FIRST OF THE MONTH   The Rabbis in the Haggadah discuss why the Passover story must be recited at night at the Seder, on the fifteenth day of the Jewish month of Nisan, rather than during the day and on the first of the month.

THE FOUR CHILDREN   Different places in the Bible use different expressions when talking about how one is supposed to tell their children about the Passover story. This is understood to mean that the story must be told differently to four different kinds of people: the wise one, the wicked one, the simple one, and the one who does not even know to ask.

THE FOUR CUPS   At each of four important parts of the Seder, it is customary to drink a cupful of wine or grape juice.

THE FOUR QUESTIONS   At the Seder it is customary for the youngest child to begin by asking a series of questions about four unusual features of the meal: why matzah and bitter herbs are eaten, why people dip their food, and why they lean when they sit.

GRACE AFTER MEALS   After every meal, it is customary to recite a blessing to thank God for the food. In Hebrew, this is called *Birkat Ha-mazon*. At the Seder, Grace is sung over a cup of wine.

HAGGADAH   Jews in each generation are commanded to tell the wonderful story of their liberation from Egyptian slavery, especially at the Seder. The traditional text that is used for this is called the *Haggadah* ("telling").

HA LACHMA   A section at the beginning of the Haggadah where we point to a piece of matzah and invite people to the Seder.

HALLEL   On festive holidays like Passover, a series of thanksgiving Psalms (from the Book of Psalms in the Bible) are recited. At the Seder, they are sung over a cup of wine.

HAMETZ   When the Israelites left Egypt, it was so sudden that the dough they took with them to make bread did not have time to rise (leaven) and become ordinary bread. To remember this, anything that contains bread or yeast, or any other leavened items must be carefully removed from Jewish homes before Passover and cannot be eaten or used during the holiday. In Hebrew, leaven is called *hametz*. Instead of hametz, Jews eat matzah during Passover.

HILLEL AND HIS SANDWICH   Hillel the Elder was one of the greatest Jewish teachers and leaders of ancient times. He tried to observe literally the Biblical command to eat the Pesah offering together with matzah and maror by combining them all together in a "sandwich."

KIDDUSH   Every Jewish holy day is officially introduced by reciting a special blessing called the *Kiddush* over a cup of wine. The Hebrew word Kiddush means "sanctification," "making holy." On Passover, it is recited at the beginning of the Seder, and it is the first of the Four Cups.

MATZAH   When the Israelites left Egypt, their dough did not have time to rise and make real bread. All they took with them were flat, dry unleavened cakes called *matzah*. In order to remember this, only matzah may be eaten on Passover, not hametz.

OPENING THE DOOR   At the end of the Seder meal, it is customary to open the door and welcome in the Prophet Elijah.

PASSOVER   (in Hebrew: *Pesah*)   The week-long Jewish holiday, occurring during the Spring season, that recalls when the Israelites, the ancestors of (present-day) Jews, were miraculously freed from centuries of slavery in Egypt. The name refers to the last of the ten plagues that God inflicted on the Egyptians. All their firstborn children were put to death, but God "passed over" the houses of the Israelites. Immediately afterward, they were set free.

PESAH   The original Hebrew word for Passover. Also refers to the lamb that was sacrificed and eaten in ancient times on the first night of the holiday.

PHARAOH   The name given to all ancient Egyptian kings, especially the wicked one who refused to allow the Israelites to go free.

RABBI AKIVA   An ancient Jewish teacher who stayed up all night telling about the wonders of how the Israelites were freed from Egypt.

RABBI ELEAZAR BEN AZARIA   An ancient Jewish teacher who tried to find a source in the Bible that said we should tell about the liberation from Egypt at night. He did not find it, but Ben Zoma did. It is said that when Rabbi Eleazar was chosen for an important position, he became so worried that his hair turned white like a seventy-year-old man, even though he was really less than twenty years old at the time.

RECLINING, LEANING   In ancient times, people at fancy feasts used to lie down on couches when they ate. Because this is the custom of free people, it is customary at the Seder to lean to one side during the meal.

SEDER   The festive meal held on the first nights of Passover. The participants recite the Haggadah, as they symbolically relive the experiences of slavery and the joy of being free people. The traditional ceremony is very complicated, so it is done according to a detailed order. The Hebrew word *Seder* means "order."

THE TEMPLE   The two great Temples of Jerusalem were the centers of Jewish worship in ancient times. The second Temple was destroyed by the Roman army in the year 70 C.E. Since then, Jews have not offered sacrifices, including the Pesah offering.

THE TEN PLAGUES   The Bible tells that Pharaoh did not give in and allow the Israelite slaves to leave Egypt until after God had inflicted upon them ten terrible plagues:

- The water turned to blood
- Lice
- Cattle disease
- Hail
- Darkness
- Frogs
- Wild animals
- Boils
- Locusts
- The deaths of all the Egyptian firstborn